FIONA CAMERON
SHE MAY BE RADON

Newton-le-Willows

Published in the United Kingdom in 2021
by The Knives Forks And Spoons Press,
51 Pipit Avenue,
Newton-le-Willows,
Merseyside,
WA12 9RG.

ISBN 978-1-912211-68-5

Acknowledgements:

'Brexit Kar Parc' and 'Perverse Strait' were first published in *Poetry Wales Vol.54 Winter 2018*

'Back and Forth' was first published in *Strix issue no.4 2018*

Supported using public funding by
ARTS COUNCIL
ENGLAND
LOTTERY FUNDED

For the Brown Bear,
The Sausage Dog
& Emyr.

.

Contents

Green Tomato Chutney

After Gillian Clarke

a letter takes the form of young tomato plants
sat fat   sweet tang   in terracotta seats
from the maternal garden in a faraway country

take this carefully
and plant it in your soil

the designated patch
the space where you will grow
the lines of creeping buttercup march
chickweed frills the soil
cat shit sometimes
pointed nettle heads droop silver coins of admonishment
willow herb weeps and scolds
and other messages emerge in the loam

but weeds are cleared
somehow
finding
        time
                to
                hack
        the
        earth
        like
        a gardener

        slapstick canery support structure
        tangles me / cat / baby /
        loose ties unravel with ease
        you grow in the wrong way
        bent and curling

        but still you grow throughout the damp summer

produce fruit
intermittently
sometimes I'm surprised
as green furry globes appear
overnight and smell like real tomatoes

there should be:
elderflower wine fermenting
nettle soup bubbling
cabbages squeaking fresh dumped in baths of steam
papery onions rolling over kitchen worktops

only tomatoes
bending stretching stinking sweet
no intervention required
September offers a window to salvage stubborn fruit

green tomato chutney
no *spiced oranges*
no *Seville orange marmalade*

just the colander rattling and bouncing with strange shaped fruit
an internet recipe I use
to tease you into sweet cauldron slop
call home faraway to find out the business of sterilisation

so now I'm cooking brittle glass

they are full
brown vacuum of sweet mess
all grown-up and ready to go home

High Meadow at Hafod

                                                                    out of the corner
                                                                of my eye there's

                                                                nothing there

                                                                honestly

there *is* the   slow curtain   call   of
        long   pine trees

hide & swish sideways to welcome us

                                                    couchy echoes
                                                    recycle still air
                                                    shhhhh shhhhhh
                                                        backstage
                                                    echo! echo! echo!

yourbreathretainsthetracesofanoutline

            forest door ajar
                                                4 x 4 folded sweet sheet meadow
                                                sown   &   regularly   hacked
                                                upholds   a   sense   of order in
                                                wildness   of   openness

our tent pitched in the centre of time

four corners twitch & buck tilting   decades trickle sideways   slide mercury

drops back to grass & roots reabsorb / reform

enter to the left:

your voices

deaden in the pine wall. Shhhhhh shhhhh shhhhhh echo! echo! echo!

thrown

to. R e a p p e a r

over your shoulder

evaporating   chattering rooks

we move

in

whispers

Three Places at Once

For Mum and Dad

animal dappled canopy
spindle fingers scratch a
pelt
waiting
at the rhododendron gate &
the sandstone capstone watches us
inhale leaf mould   (specifically damp oak and dry pine)

                        bats & purple velvet interiors
                        Victorian you will say &
                        you would be wrong.

witch's house & thick sugar lattice
turquoise drainpipe snakes

oh layers!

shedding rotten patterns drop
undress to the opaque winter

            Strait shelf curdle moss, wood & soil in
            cold hicking bubbles
            water breaking clods apart

                                        high tennis courts eaten by fern & ivy
                                                                        maybe
                                        only exist in the travelling mind

                                        I am fairly sure it is *not* OK
                                to play Hansel & Gretel with your kids
                                                                in a forest

return to these autumns   in bits
& pieces
scent & fragment
wood & toadstool air
sleep & carbohydrates

                                  low Sunday sun / gas fire heat rash

                                  sticks   trailed   silently   through

                                  silver sand deposits

Gap

writing in the gap between the cat's teeth
                   and bands of afternoon sun
     passing
        time
            in the shallows
                  of the lower half of the clock
       pooling in the tepid time   after lunch

     charting a continent at the kitchen worktop
        tracing crumb
            to crumb
                mimics connections
       elsewhere

waiting for you after school
in the condensation window of Advent
          just opening
November dead behind us
                  we never get anything done round here
afternoons lost to the phone screen
peering into other worlds

school has a foyer
full of frost & steam
& papier-mâché islands
confectionery atolls
glitter-glue oceans &
bubble wrap snow wastes
            Lapland silent in cork & felt
       penguins versus barley sugar whirls

Ynys Môn reconfigured in poster paint and a
gargantuan golf course   straddles the land mass

the children are overexcited and confused

in an empty classroom
abandoned A4 sheet shows scrawl of black shiny
comedy bomb with fuse
collides with a bent Eiffel tower
speech bubble shrieks 'oh no!'

I know they had guns you say later
some of the kids didn't understand
they thought it was a bomb…

lines   make   their   way   home
                    dinner cooks itself
you're playing a game
                    we're going on a journey before dinnertime
I listen behind a door

Hoylake

Imagine how the space will look once painted   it's not just about how it

will appear to others it's about how it   will *make you feel inside*

inner heart it's about   it's because it's such a
magical colour it's   a rough stack of gorse

silver bath tap tiles   pool light

swimming in your bath   sourced Murano
blue   parrots / palms

it doesn't fit   makes itself
difficult   wide-eyed   frank and
     open   sand

sand piling and piling and piling at the end   of Merseyside streets

before school   after school and sand in
dreams and sand   in sheets and sandstone which is
rose pink round here   sometimes and confuses
me and sand in the theatre   and sinking sand stealing
shoes

and the red geraniums   in hot terracotta this is the
sign of a home that is   working this is the sign
and scent of a home   that is working in the 1980s and a
mother's light   denim dungarees this is the sand running
over and over   and minding the neighbour's dog
         she only owns one record
         which astounds me Brideshead

Revisited soundtrack   and the dog which is a collie comes to the beach
a lot with us   and pulls away and snaps at ankles and we love her
because   we think she is ours to have

in the storm over the Mersey   tide wriggles and   crawls in

curling our ankles

8pm summer night   lapping tongue tide and warning
us warning us   too quiet and purple   sky ecclesiastical
green

       silence and crack   the dog pulls us home

                     in time to see the church tower struck

A Spell at Blaenau

when we walk together
the roads are satin ribbons
tearing air
you float in silvery pools
hovering through town

navigating the rock face at every street corner
unseen paintings continue to go unseen
beneath the rock

children still have to run away from home

we   bounce   steps
no matter what the terrain   beneath
when the pavement is wet with golden slate
water runs like fuel in the streets
I am starting to learn its signs

as we circle the town
higher up
we're two foxes in bracken
chasing around inside each other's language
from here to there
I can see clearly the way the stone of the home lies
horizontal
the painted white lintel of every window
smiling deep shafts in sunlight
the thin veil
between the indoors and the out
sure that somewhere along this line of roads
I have been tricked

Annual Domestic

the radio voice in   some other room   talks about
women

from   two   whole   days
away

I hear you

walk bedroom floorboards &
marvel at the stasis   set in cold   frozen warning
fingers of winter already claw at the dressing table
a fine film of dust settled gently on perfume bottle edge
bed sheets cold and limp to the touch
                                        the dead have visited and left
          the tip of my nose – a separate thing
what we can't see   hangs in the air

banished by the   yellowwarmthofnoise
the setting of the fire
making people shaped dips in cold sofas
kettles rushing to the boil
walls stretching and life reasserting

light falls in the same places every year / makes the same shadows sway

Corris Police House, Meirionnydd 1966

baby bottle metronome
kept time under the clouds
footsteps measured other worlds thudding sunk on the valley floor
prams wheels turned seconds then minutes into hours and days
near icy rivers glowing with rust

you made sure that nobody knew
you were
           sunk

Corris Police House

walked my fingers along Braich Goch spine   mapping

50 years later   I'm   pressing   my story   against yours
                        stitching your shadow to mine
                                        unpicking time

conjuring the exhalation of long plumes
satisfied forest steam
&
                        woodsmoke snakes whispering out
                        high amongst pine teeth gaps
                        I pressed your skin with my image of the past

        c'mon spit it out

                                        tapping insistently on present glass
hoping to see your breath mist

                        your skin colouring under my thumb print

I'm making a mark now
                in the contours of my throat
I can't help it
                tumbles   out   like   music

weeds sprout in   untended memory

The First Night: Police House #2*

For Ellen

first sharp falls of icing sugar air   dance over
plump baby fists
the days ahead   tilt toward Christmas

and home is now   no home
     magnolia walls
fresh chilled cream

and doors hours wide open as a shop

     something somewhere
twitches at memory lodged inside walls

removal men   now nervous   fumble hurriedly in the grate
a fire appears   a parting gift
they abandon ship   into the night   the clink and slosh of pubs and people

tŷ unnos

whether you wanted it or not
smoke rose from the chimney before the sun set and
you have been admitted
               to this mess

---

* Note: In the winter of 1967 my mother and father-in-law (a police officer) were transferred to a new police house
  after the previous officer in residence murdered his wife, two daughters, the dog and then took his own life.

Fiona Cameron

Highlight

salt & wind

batters thin glass   in frames

high whooping   sheets of grey nothing   snap across city lines

                 seagull turns air flinty

on sky fragments

                        folded descent into

golden sun bath

Back and Forth

in the kitchen
the sea is as
quiet as the street
at dawn

it laps and curls
in teacup shattered light.

      sand   drifts in the sink
& your empty shoes
      climb
          sandstone
                 stoops

in silence
      at 6.05 am
the cat's   arch   opens the
day & when

the radio speaks

I reply

Fiona Cameron

Separate Parts of Midsummer's Eve 2015

next shoes mummy?
bedtime?
swallowed by the curtain hole

why is?
why?
why is why?

Why am I?
inclined toward the star that it orbits

the air in this room is exactly the same temperature as the blood in your veins
desire wobbles in invisible air

carwash   carwashes   carwash
brushes

what is there over there?

what is the over there?

what is behind that?

the sun is going?
a sun is going away

the sun is going away

flows   currents   beats
softest blanket falters momentarily on hot feet

on your back   on the tilt of a planet   drift   under purple heather fall

into the last eruption of the year
the sun in splendour
shadow and star toppled

position yourself in the sky
tripping over one another
to race for the prize

Fiona Cameron

The Field at Dusk

orange humming the rose hour sky

        we   are   moving

        back

on child foot   tracking hoof   bounding   hopping

          tracking   dew spattered blades

        on tip-toes   reverse of

I am moving down between hedgerow   and under white blast

        of hawthorn

        between then

        and now

        look!

          the past lies   around the corner of the field where the

        shadow just fell   see?

the winter sun cleaves an exit   bows out like a traitor   and I feel you're

        back with me   now   under dry rooted oak face

a century's height/width   irrelevancies again   again

Perverse Strait

gravel gives way / saves
sliding feet soles down
to an eruption of edges
/ it is inevitable & steep

it is tempting & why
not? / after all /

it is only blue-ness &
deep green rope weed / that
bind paprika crabs &

it is only the soft underside of the
iridescent / the coy moon
bottomed out at the
point where white sand
gasps in secret

come on in and fill up to
the cold finger-line
stroke of your waist /
let sun radiate arms &
off-shore breeze knock
your hair & neck cold
/ blink blank sun
surrender / & watch /
watch / watch the
current / charm your silly snake legs
/ & pull at your glittering head

Brexit Kar Parc

par cark tone bumps   music to time travel to

beat dancing in disobedient   tapestry stitch   ratcheting up a mess of scribble on every
single surface

flush through silver after chemical wash of rain streaks and   air our acid dirty laundry
          in our own bloody back yard

every car is crying regret

all coats in shining seal grey smudged   traffic cone outrageous orange
stands warning/unheeded

through half shut eyes

and then again   lighthouse wave   light again   milky warning
again and again   retina blank

a singer coos in argent   like

metal dove talk   &   perhaps

I am going to transport the thick granite of the head
                    heave dead ideas over clifftops single handed

Anabranch

a foot strikes desperate at
billowing
      nothingness

anticipate space   already available

      planned for erasure
got ahead of yourself again

brick wall softens

Tablet 1: Preliminary Notes

dreamt of dinosaurs ripping up the park

again

thanks for the feedback

not meaning it

Tuesday? why use it?

read my book

before I've started it

no additional text

pair of eyes caught   between   swimming cap

and pool edge

new note: 1 sketch

new note: 1 sketch

new note: 1 sketch

arrange a meeting with the desired outcome

weirdo-kind

list every colour of green in a vista

and clean the bathroom

twice

a town called malice

collect flutes

boiler service

and the Shiant Islands

take: Hoover/Windolene/sheets

Dogville – chalk – our town out quickly ahead of the troubles

PLAN

The Island of Girls takeover

1 banana / 3 coffees / tuna mayonnaise sandwich

drown book now

pizza and crisps

Zone E / Row 3 / Green Zone (DO NOT get lost)

this is an appeal I simply shouldn't have to make

more black jeans

KJ08 WYS (IMPORTANT)

Deliberate misspelling

Vulpine elaborate

Laiva

Dorothea

Melancholia

Vivien

Moheda

To Do: no additional text
lamb mince
Ischia: Bay of Naples
hidden lumber room
where?

Orlop Deck?
Nelson…that church
Lake Enchanto

washing powder – get
nappies
sausages
low self-esteem
short and galvanised
EVP
Microbit
shadow of death without any order
apple
I don't know who you are yet
goat: no additional text
((((the telling of the bees))))
Jonathan Becker, *Carriage, Paris 1978*
Maquette /Ergo/ Bumbo
Spiderland
Atomised
This house protects dreaming

Tablet 2: The Quarry Pit and a Matter of Time

Dorothea basks
in freshwater salts
under the black and crag slate conversations

hacked out a mountain

they say you can see the quarries
from space

there is under shudder in
dark rooms of

navy water
under shudder in there

skirt the pit at dusk and watch the surface   see

scraped another plane on the earth's face

they're coming up again

Tablet 3: Minecraft Realms 2034

surface fissures stemming from irresponsible fracking practice in the early 2000s   lead to deeper
        worldwide rents and tears

north America was irreparably swollen and blistered in a multitude of locations   the land mass of northern Europe shuddered frequently

now   & flapping wounds appeared in numerous south American valleys   the African continent was splitting near Equatorial Guinea's

border with Cameroon

        Bioko and other volcanic areas   were considered a great risk

it

        inevitably lead to   explorative attempts within the Minecraft™ realm to get certain groups

coded, ghosted and sent underground

        children experts were often called upon to assist transition   to help dig our   way out

one way or another   we just kept on digging

governments generally felt it was perfectly reasonable and quite possible to leave it to the children   who knew more anyway
        but it was hard for a lot of people of a certain age

to accept it really would end like this   naturally, if you were significantly older   it was   hard to breach to the two
        worlds with

belief & ease   the children just slipped through

Tablet 4: Cloudy Borderline

purple/melyn   drone dancing now

tide sound   missing fire

rain in   rain out   Brexit red

above shoemaker's silk   heave cloudy blankets

rain & tides   tides & rains

            tides & rains

god! these times…

the soft throwing strang of the cold organ

wheeze &

sheets sail in sky alleys   & again
this parodic beat again & again & again

bent forms wash the frost wind in puddle days

& cardigans runnel hard

in grey brick back yards

game boys sea-shiver & in trees

the fresh sluice

    of sap is needed daily now

Tablet 5: Snap

dreaming of dinosaur jaws ripping up the park
again
of your teeth becoming a smiling brittle honeycomb   and the
chasm of black jaw
          gaped   as teeth exploded
into cosmic fathoms

watch this!   scroll---------   scroll   scroll---------   scroll   thumb it
spooling out of control like digital microfiche   unwinding upon warm carpet   consult lunar systems

Pokémon characters wobble and interrupt the space like acid bubbles

we return to the medieval axe and stake
flames folding over skin
children lying in the rubble of the town square
a petrol station ablaze in the snappy air of a numb   November night

          our way of life coming to an end in our lifetime

Tablet 6: By June I'd Given Up and Given Over to Magic

and obviously

because we are worn   down   to desperate magic   we

transform the children into giddy

young mountain goats

so as to avoid danger

the inevitable draft

& death

Tablet 7: The Telling of the Bees at the End

go   go quickly when   to the nearest hive
the time comes
within 8 miles

for us   that's the cottage in ------   remember, I told you? It's written down too.

don't panic   yet   just make sure you

hang the hive with the black cloth

speak calmly   clearly   if you can

sudden movement and noise will frighten them   hush now   hush

                                              remember what I told you to say

Fiona Cameron

Tablet 8: Michael Flatley's Private Inauguration Dance for Donald and Melania Trump

For Mary Rita

on TV
we never saw

the incessant flicker of rubber limbs in
full bullion flow
and the cracking of lamé heels on marble
spinning snapping eventually
becoming invisible as he disintegrates and then
ignites

The End

Tablet 9: 'I have a massive, unshakeable feeling that our way of life will come to an end in my lifetime. It's unsustainable. I keep it to myself.'

information is buzzing, swarming. the air is constantly dragged down. the world turns quite funny right now. fractured. cracked open.

repetition beats on tired ears. I have an unshakeable feeling. in my lifetime... there's anxiety spilled on this carpet. cutlery pares

down options. I've stopped going down to the sea. the arrows are in movement now. flashes of grit in the stars. in the back of time –

snagging. he says mummy. mummy. when I had a different mummy. before the fire came from the sky. magnify, then step away. mainly volcanoes exert critical force. islands do tend to sheer off. head first. flatten all thought. paralytic time. I have an unshakeable feeling. tangled, looped, re-treading. he says, mummy, mummy, who will feed the cats? fragile rose rock pools hold light universes. answers in yellow shallows. someone plays a tape in another room, then another, then another. we have made a loose and casual arrangement to meet ourselves coming back sometime. choreography of the collective unconscious is precarious. I have an unshakeable feeling. it blooms at night in some minds.

in others, on a sweet clear afternoon near the sea.

Tablet 10: A Thousand Cycles to Come

Juncker's vineyard is fucked anyway

pick: fire

    water

        or war

Nico's harmonium plays an endless counterpoint to

        the plane drone in the mountains nr here

it's the sound of defeat

it's a Monday in the 21st century

there are spiders in my pockets

and Brexit on the radio

it's the sound of pop

people do something like working or

dancing

spiders curl in my pockets

office heels click on lino   hammers hit wood

someone types something somewhere else

sounds like work

sounds like work

sounds something like work
old fashioned
like working
or dancing

there are worms in my hair

Hitler's Inner Circle of Evil streams forever
on Netflix

there are cobwebs between my fingers
the door of no.10 bangs all night in the wind

whether or not whether or not whether or not

are you coming or going?

Tablet 11: Lone House / West Wales Coastal Marshland / 2033

you find it harder to
unhear the ringing on the marshes
these days

are   starting earlier   waking in the screaming hours before dawn   daybreak

the baby blue and the baby pink horizon rubs flat cheeks against
persistent at the pane

as something unburies itself   again   and   again   in   your   line   of   sight

out there   metallic reeds rattle something of flight
&

somewhere   in the stomach collective   fluttering like fish

a warm lie flips
restless

The Missing Manifesto

all of it
every last scrap
inside the corners of dreams
and drains
at the back of caves
centuries unseen
drip black
a chalky buried brick
in the Berlin bombsite
a last resort
on holiday
a can of Heinz baked beans
lying
prone on the moon
come in through the backdoor
leave by the front
you think I
won't cross you
on the stairs?
it takes a village to raise a child
into what?
a towering inferno?
leap / a frog / a golden ball
dropped to
the bottom of a well

Fiona Cameron

Under Adda Alive

when we flipped the cathedral over
steeple spikes the mud
flimsy ideas   idle in the backwash   shared a sewer
overused and a bit tired   nosediving in the ebb
tugging a shale-filled sock in the flow
unseen ripples   causing   then   uncausing   unseen   effects
exist in the reverse of imagination
unceasing   rushes same   clump of weed   over years
and the Buddhists say something about time elapsing so slowly…
boulder kalpa
I forget   about the ferns   that always proliferate   in the gaps
upper vaults of cavern reversed in the water course
thrums to the beat of the   tarmac   tongue   above
in the bit between whatever   and Next   confined water shudders tight
barrelling   hums
until   uncurls   silver cutlery temple   hung with slime   receives
an air-bound explosion of spray   in backwards proscenium
subterranean city ballroom   echoes a traffic dance   bellow
stock sits sunk flat and redundant   on the valley floor
sound decays to a pinprick
viewed through a manhole cover   by a child

Walks: Moon-Side of the Botanical Gardens (Between Britannia and Menai Bridges)

Day 1

Moon phase: waxing crescent
Tide phase: ebb
Time: 13.15

something fawn and winged

      springs   air   under-bent

wax-leaf canopy   celestial drips

         up against it

walk at a pace pushing back against invisible weight of brined water rush below

salt water leaving the skin cells now   &   tide race drinking Menai bed
      skeletal   dry

      moon withdrawal

blood fill void / push and pull and empty in glistening thickets from freshwater

rain   smiling underfoot

Day 2

Moon phase: waxing crescent
Tide phase: flow
Time: 12.40

Strait   is moving   too fast
like satin ribbons cutting air

rapid surface tension exists only to trick you
it did   your eyes play an impossible game of   catch-up

footsteps bound over each other to parallel the haphazard rhythm below

Day 3

Moon phase: waning
Tide phase: ebb
Time: 11.22

big Baltic blue   spreads fast   ranging wide   too quickly   to
understand

one   frill   of   lace   water   trails   from   high   tide   marker
      stuck like a twig in storm drain
after rain

brewing & fizzing in the crucible of the
fault line   as time catches up with itself and out spills in crazy
incoherent directions

at Britannia stanchion   I'm too scared to look down

Day 4

Moon Phase: Waxing
Tide phase: ebb
Time: 2.45

catch the smell of yourself

yesterday

between warm autumn years

still to arrive

a grey linen seagull song

moves at angles

down / along / between the Strait

over train engine howl

in bridge tunnel hole

spitting raw stone and metal

knitted   sounds   float

landing as a cloak on

uneasy shoulder

as feet hit repeat   soil and leaf

my shoulders

alight & touch

then fall underfoot

warning layers   emerge

a chattering of folds and corners & forgotten rooms

don't look back

at the tree tunnel

the seagull call is just a recording

Day 5

Moon phase: waning
Tide phase: ebb
Time: 11.45

today there are children

huddled in stick-built dens   forest school

all eyes
all watching
all glinting

bamboo   flecked   sunlit eaves

stretched stretching weight against whittle
and poised to
fight

they hunch
glower red

hey!   you!

turning in the dense leaf cover mud smeared cheekbone catches leopard light in the canopy

the teacher comes to lead them back

Day 6

Moon Phase: waning crescent
Tide phase: flow
Time: 14.38

      rare &

                                    explicit

                  light
      pockets

      bold / ceremonial / baroque

      the Strait
      a fat coil
      a gold brocade

Day 7

Moon phase: waxing
Tide phase: flow
Time: 12.15

           tent

                triangle

sun   wriggle   on   sea

repetitive eating at the cusp of land   as tight as crystal cuts

        paddle a flat & dumb response

launch   hurl   empty   yourself

                     in this   soaking mystery

Day 8

Moon phase: waning
Tide phase: ebb
Time: 11.11

after   and   even
during the rain washing
it felt like it was over at moments
it did &
it was still falling over
and over & the woods were
playing keen slant tricks &
of water & silver earth
I smelt myself over and over

Fiona Cameron

Fingers in the Plug

bare bones of a beginning & short changing those who might stick around

everyone's in the garden anyway   go through

                how do you know it's even possible?   *it's a sort of feeling...*

like under the turf   of the lino   of everyday life

it's always there   you can   tune in at   some point   I think

like the carpets in *Where the Wild Things Are*

lush   grass   jungle   &   vineshungallaround

                &

sometimes the airing cupboard door   creaked & talked

forest back at you

you know   right?

that night thing   as a child

to get up   leave feathers   pillows   dolls   soft

swirled carpets

pincushion lawns   & dew meant bare feet sliced inwards of the dawn there was a garden

hanging sharp white   in black blossom and cotton sheets

a boundary collapsed here and there   I tried to cross it

every night

Fiona Cameron

She May Be Radon

she may be radon
at the January gate
the centre of it all
at the centre of it all
in the washing machine
drum
grin
rests the bone hood skull

humdrum & colander rattle
in the deathly fridge

beat-stop – shakedown – 4am

she is at the centre of it all
the hall light is
left on all night
a wardrobe door waits
ajar

she is carpet text
wriggling numerals
code the floor
she is attics
waiting to be filled

and the floorboards crack
at the centre of it all
where
the internal
 sea gawps
&
the sky split
inside

Field 1: Buried Treasure

        eye   pits   meet

            resting

brow   to   brow
crown   to   crown

bony air chain links bare air to clod   &   equal loops of space

heave   rough   breath

and   unsaid   words   that
    uncurl

unfixed in time

for the ribs to grin

their message again & it's a long long time

coming up

Field 2

is pegged in & out of time &
four corners to the winds
& livestock untethered
wander
criss cross universes

Merry-Go-Round

you're silent

eyelashed cheeks

I count years on fingers

I speculate on greasy dust
touch warm wet flannels
colour   egg yolk
powdery bubbles in bath
fleece blankets
sweet pink
sleep scent

of course
we settle grooves
knitting lines of energy
wearing wood floors smooth
polishing banisters

you touch the sill
          I the cot

changes your faces

creases up at the corners

Fiona Cameron

Deserted Noon

After Lolly Willowes

dog bark   empty pail   sound thrown like   gravel   across   time

yard

orchard

like dusk

midday blind

like the start of the night

you will wait under star

sweet anticipation

ripe treat

orchard

spell

Freedom of Movement

For Evan and Arthur

I will need your ticket, passport and visa. say: can I come through?
no
what is your name?
Evan
no, that's my name
I come from Australia
where do your wheels come from?
South Africa
where does your dummy come from?
POINTS AT MOUTH
that's not specific
how old is your cat?
90.10
how old is your dad?
96
where did you get this bin lorry from?
south Africa
what year were you born in?
year 11
stickers?
from that shop?
up there?
what country?
Australia
Wales
headlights?
South Africa
from the south?
come through NOW!
WAIT…
exactly how old is your cat?
36
90.10

cat is 90.10?

how old are you?

I need to see your passport

you can't come through. wrong visa

hold on

I think you can come through now

WAIT!

how old is your dog?

come through

WAIT!

where did your car come from?

Australia

passport

OK

WAIT! GET BACK IN!

I want to know where these two came from

India?

WAIT!

do you know what day it is?

Sunday

no. yes

you came back through. you have to answer now

I want to know how old your bottom is

26

oh no! it's nostalgic Bill the naughty criminal!

one last question

this is Brittany you idiot!

no, it's South Africa

quick! security! after that bin lorry!

& The Curve That Flew

cradles an absence

label says 'barn owl'
not 'barn owl wings'

doesn't mention absence
the stiff
fan of bone folded business
papers
a sheath of deathly chalk

or how the splash of maple
speckles   mimic bark &
vaults keratin arcs

doesn't mention the eruption
of soft grey down   that marks the
shear point of
wing limb from
body

the full moon &
the field mouse

& the curve that once
flew

Fiona Cameron

Ouija Me! Me!
For Katy and Nancy

Ouija! Ouija! singing in the back-bedroom airing cupboard in the long back-bedroom
there's a ghost in there
        I say

ghost!

do you hear me   ghost?
don't you hear me   ghost?
                hello?
                    hello?
always singsingsinging   hello!   clearing air   like bell harmonics

we wallpaper in rose, thorn and trellis
weave belief into the walls & fabric

we marvel again and again
at the glass harmonica housed in the Williamson Gallery
& its
cut crystal crank
that opens other worlds sharp
with music

we access the loft space
calling down from den to friend to
making a ouija board from A4 paper and stubby
felt tip with fat glass tumbler
Irn Bru dregs may disrupt the flow of
water tuned wine glass

O! please please please help us come unstuck!

tap tables impatiently

… hello ghost
you're very welcome
more than welcome… anytime

no answer
it's not there
you're not concentrating hard enough
now

you're moving your hand

Fiona Cameron

Open House

For Jasmin

unseen   mass   open   arms

me!
she said
it   was   me!

            they raised

            from top stair to bottom

never   touched   a   step

            it's a levitation!   oh layers!

deserts of carpet   and static from TV

crackling below

treading air   floating secrets   near the ceiling
        propelled in warm dust currents

they lifted me and I flew every day
past wallpaper blooms and houseplant vines

she said that

nobody ever saw her

she said

So Very Extraordinary

come on back in &
get explicit this time
sticky with the
truth of it & how
it's all like pointless metalwork
how wrenching & sorting the
sprung coils
of home, kids, work & money is
like fighting bull rushes
is intransigent work
is a rust orange bullshit rush
waste of time   flower
rearranging velour cushion work is
your game
a shit macramé approach to
this Instagram home
we sought
now &
steady now steady still steady
pays so little
in
in give & a lot in
take take take
don't touch that!
rose gold ornament – no thanks
copper pan talk
talk talk & breathe & breathe & breathe